MY BEST FRIEND FRED

Booksurge

Copyright 2017

ISBN-13:978-1463565138

ISBN-10:1463565135

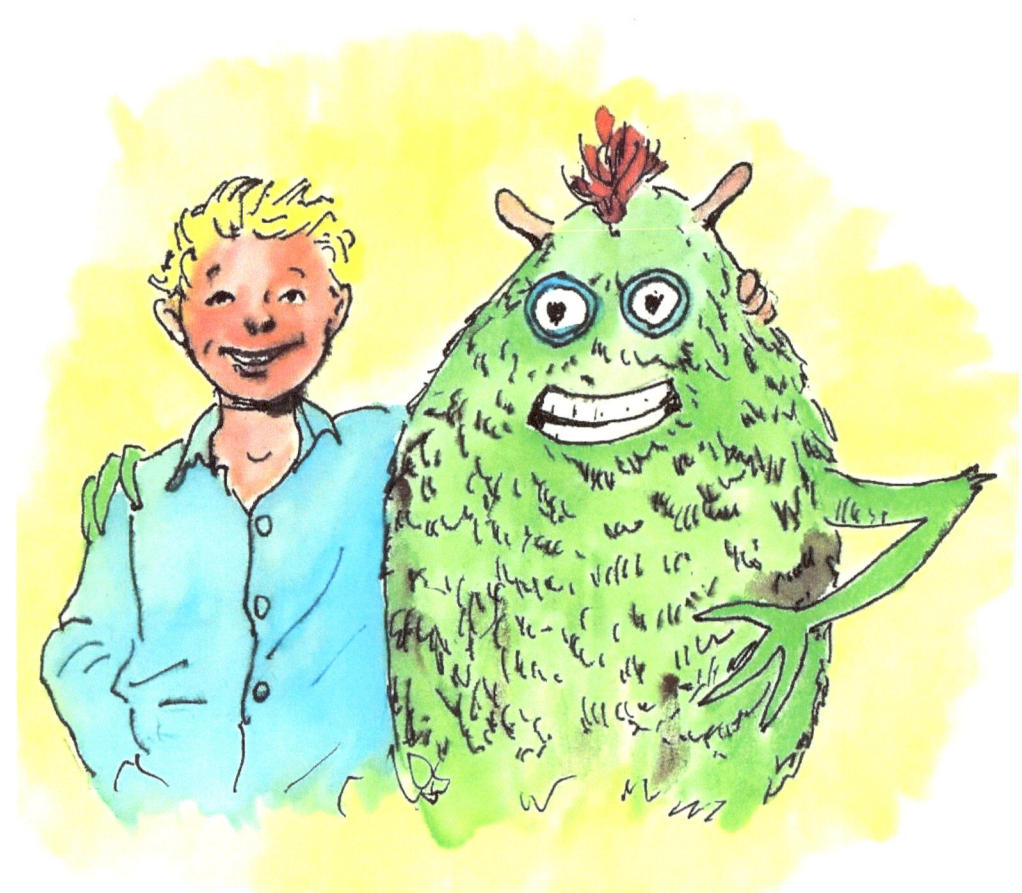

Dedications

This Book is dedicated to my Father, Earl R. Fuller. A man of true character. His talent will carry on through the generations. I thank him for teaching me that I could do anything I put my mind to. He stood behind me for all of it. THANK YOU, DAD!

My Mother, Carol J. Fuller (Langworthy) For standing behind me all my life and giving the courage to do all I wanted to do. With a gentle nudge when I needed it.

My husband Charles E. Webster, for being my best friend, greatest supporter and love of my life.

My daughter, Moriah, for how to stay a child at heart and look for the fun things in life.

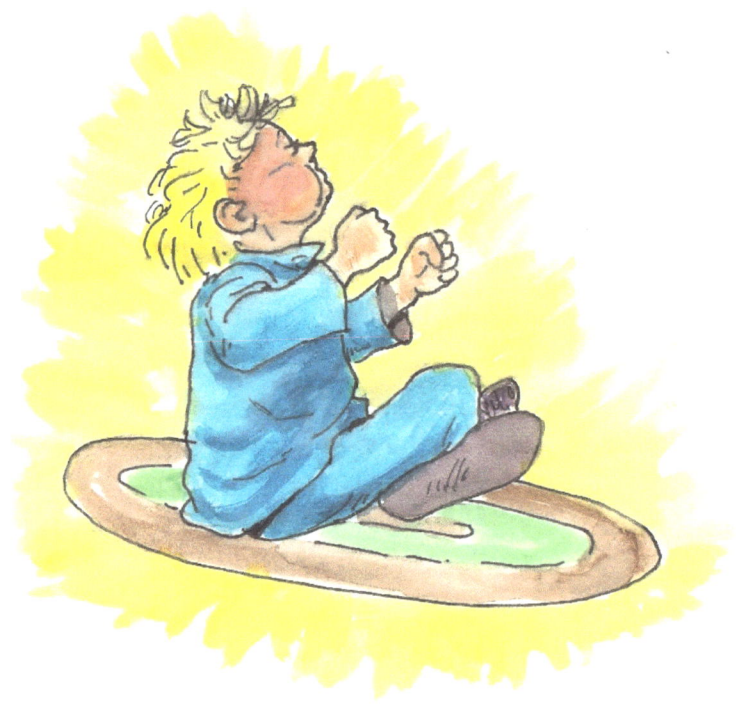

Once upon a time there was a little boy named Johnny, he hated to go to bed. He would jump up and down and throw a tantrum. He would hold hid breathe until his face turned red.

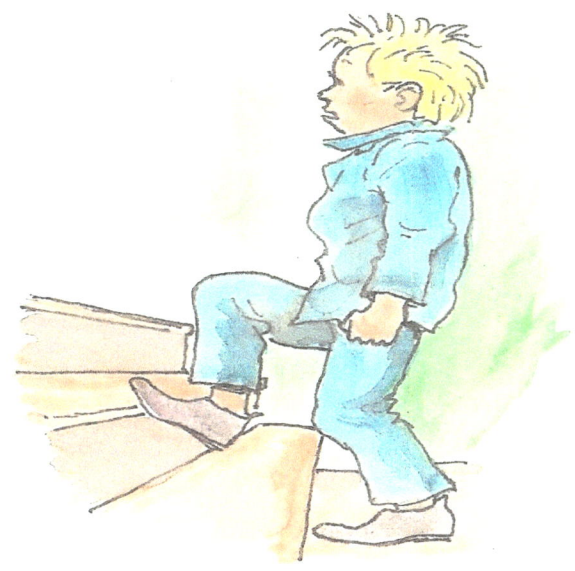

Night after night he would stomp upstairs. He would fight about and fight about it, he didn't care.

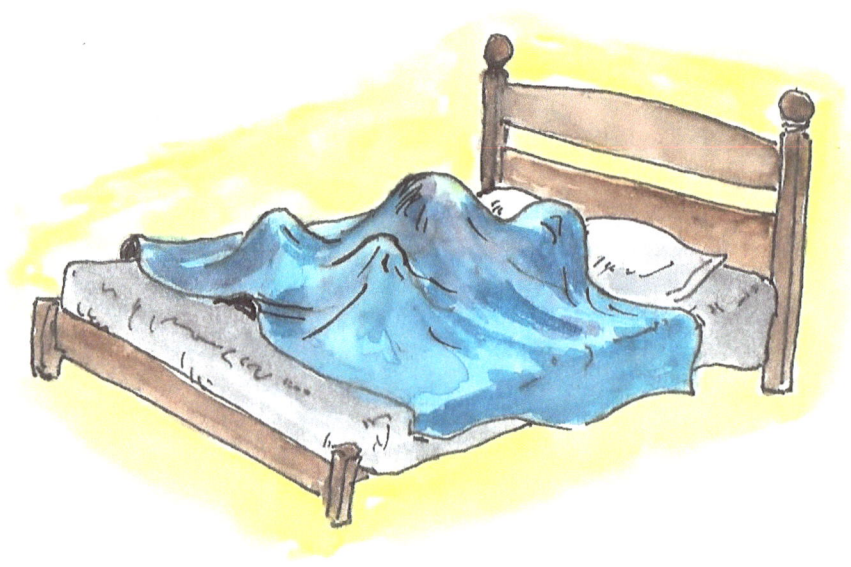

So, one night when he finally went to bed, he climbed under the sheets and covered his head.

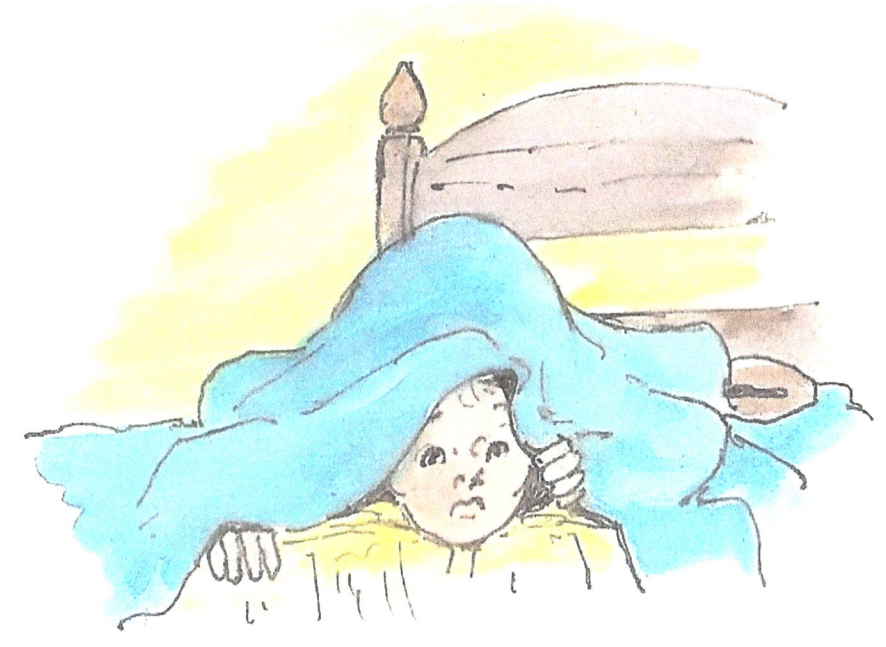

Then without warning there came a funny sound, he peeked out from under the covers; you'll never guess what he found.

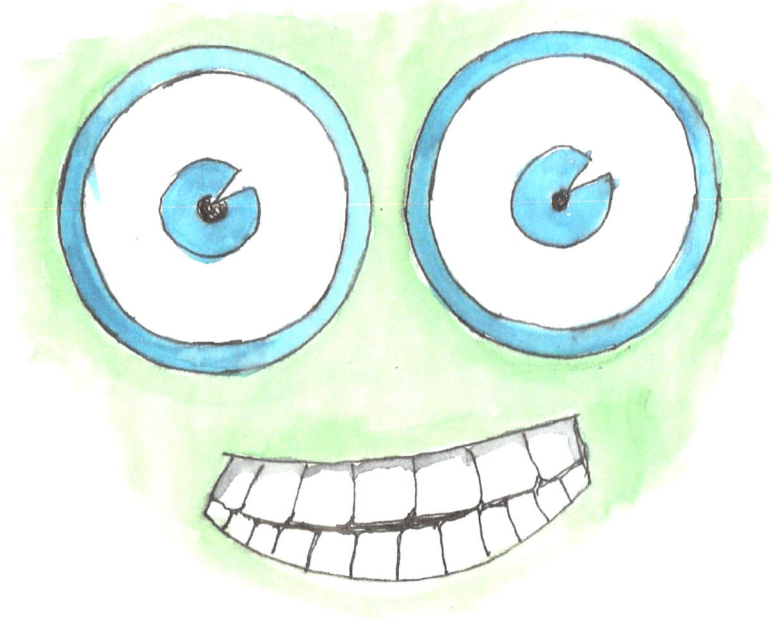

A pair of big blue eyes looking back at him. "HELLO" he heard it say with a big toothy grin.

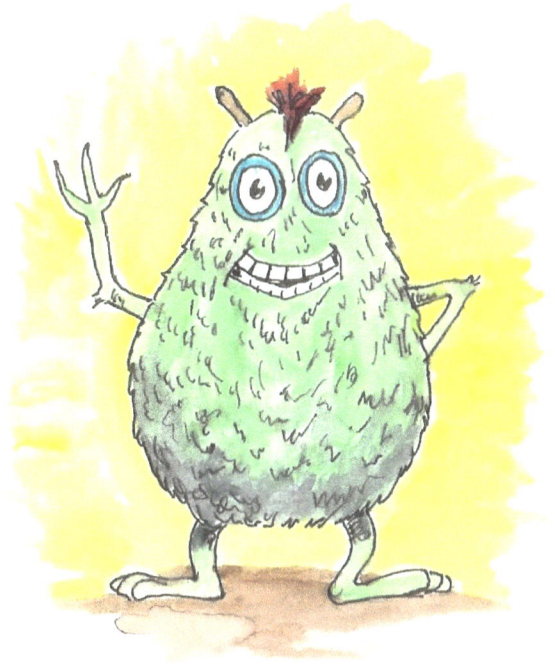

The creature was big, fuzzy, and green. But, when Johnny looked at him he didn't seem to mean. He had pointy red hair on top of his head; he looked at Johnny again and "HI! MY NAME IS FRED"

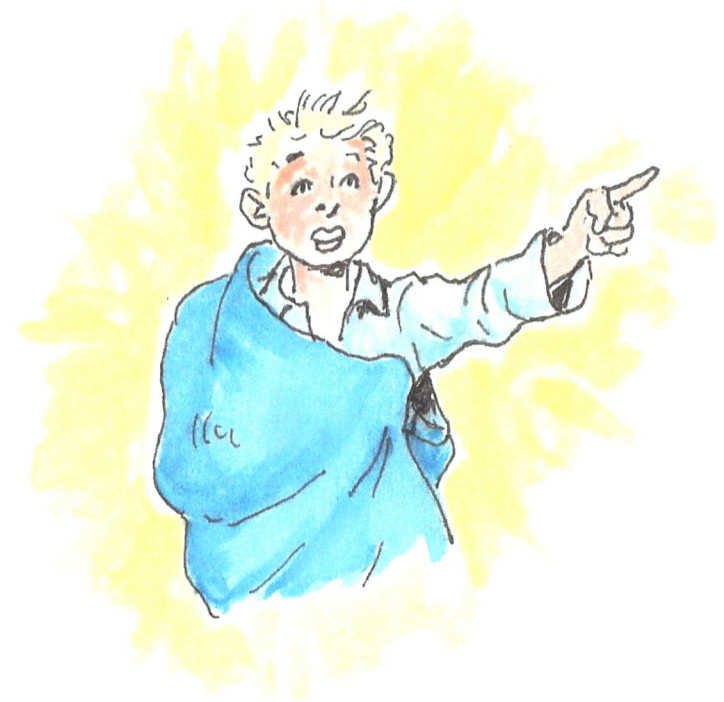

Johnny was scared, he didn't know what to say. Then he pointed at him and said "YOU CAN NOT STAY HERE,GO AWAY!"

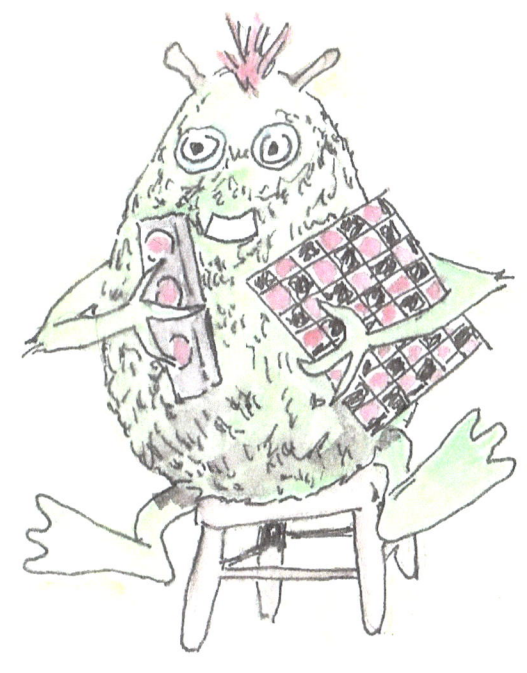

"I JUST GOT HERE." He said "WHAT DO YOU MEAN GO AWAY? I WAS HOPING THAT YOU WOULS WANT TO STAY UP AND PLAY."

"WE COULD PLAY CHECKERS OR JACKS." He said, "ANY KIND OF GAMES......."

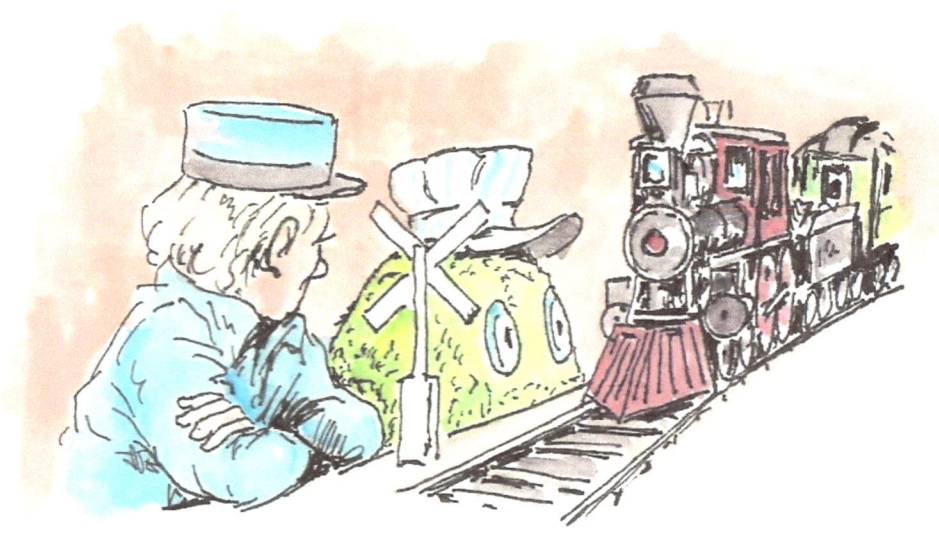

"WE COULD PRETEND" he said with a grin "WE ARE CONDUCTORS
ON A TRAIN."

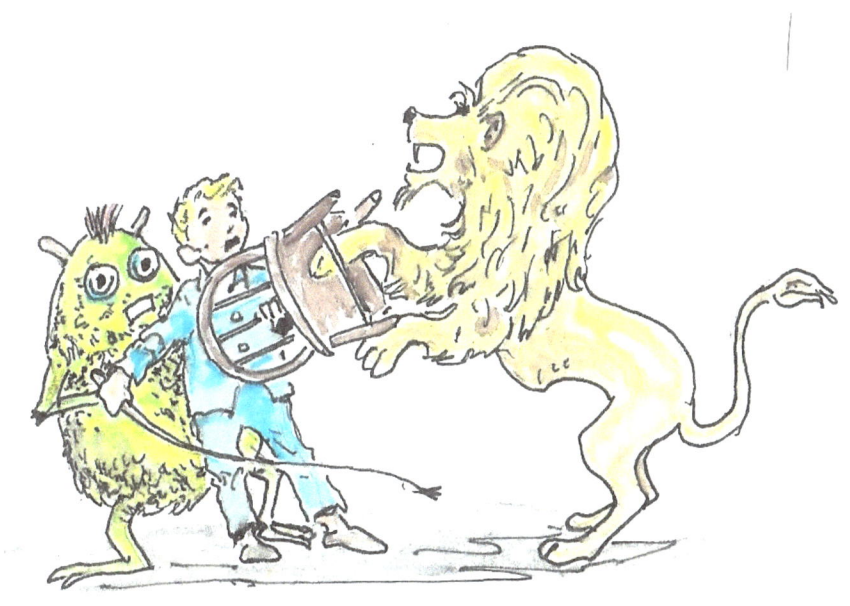

"WE CAN PRETEND WE ARE IN A CIRCUS TRAINING LIONS WITH A CHAIR."

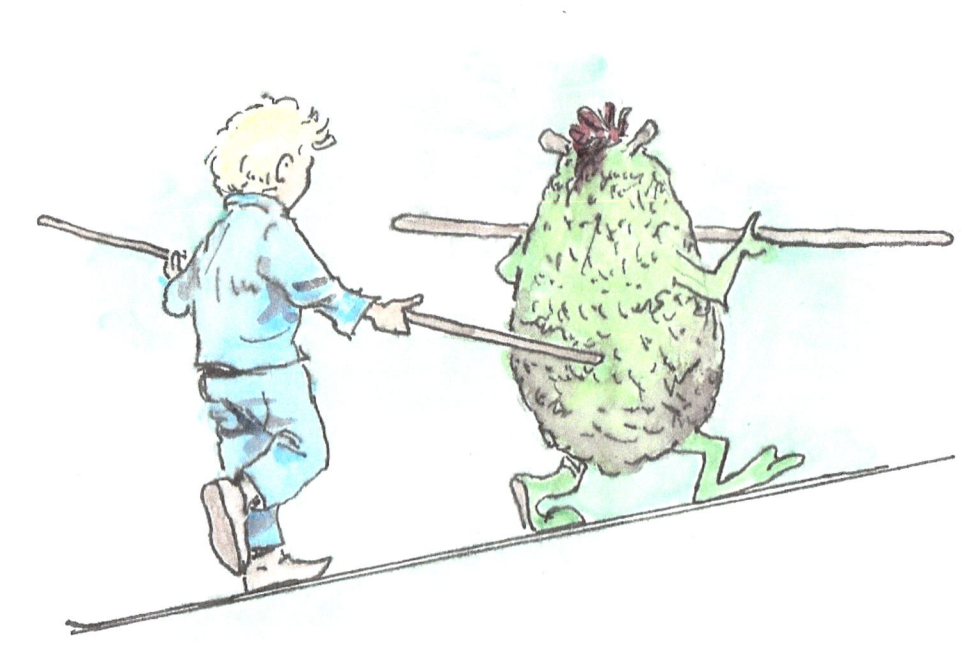

"OR WALKING ON A TIGHTROPE WAY UP IN THE AIR."

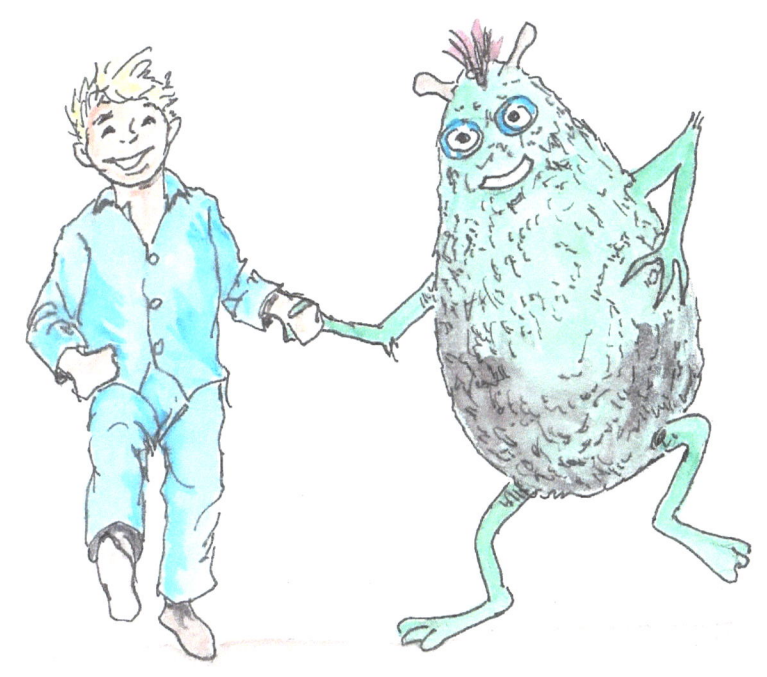

"WHERE EVER WE GO, WHATEVER WE DO" he said "YOU KNOW
IT'S MORE FUN WHEN YOU DO IT WITH TWO."

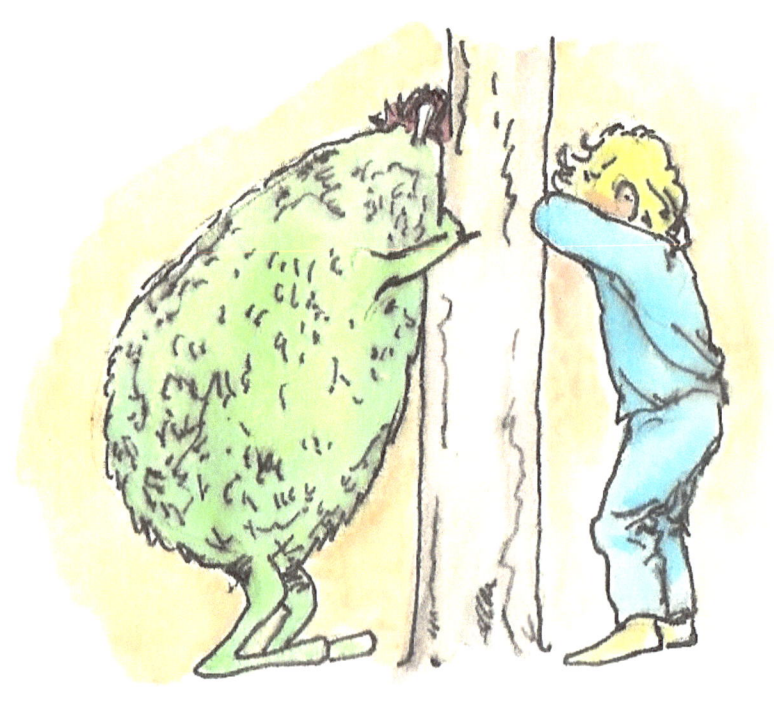

"THEN IF YOU WANT WE CAN PLAY HIDE AND SEEK."

"BUT, WE BOTH HAVE TO PROMISE THAT NEITHER WILL PEEK."

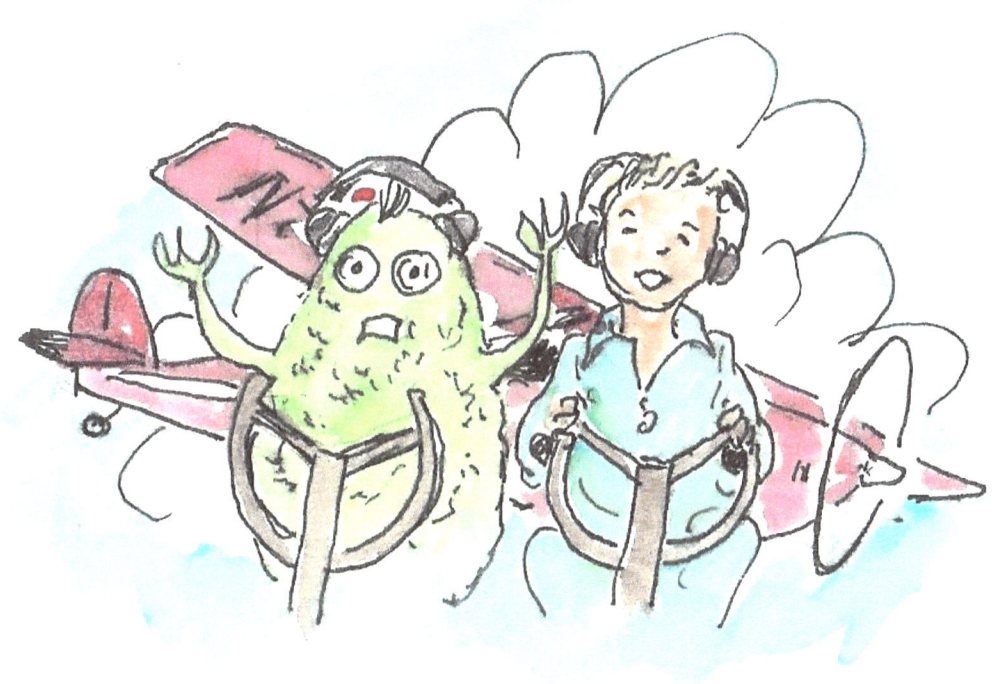

They played and they played all through the night. They even pretended they were pilots of a plane and took flight.

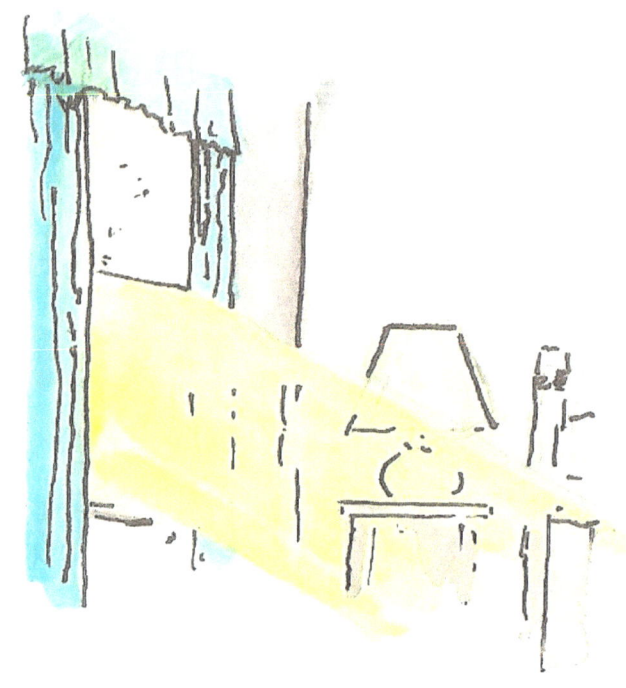

But, while they were playing and so having much fun, they didn't see through the window, up came the sun.

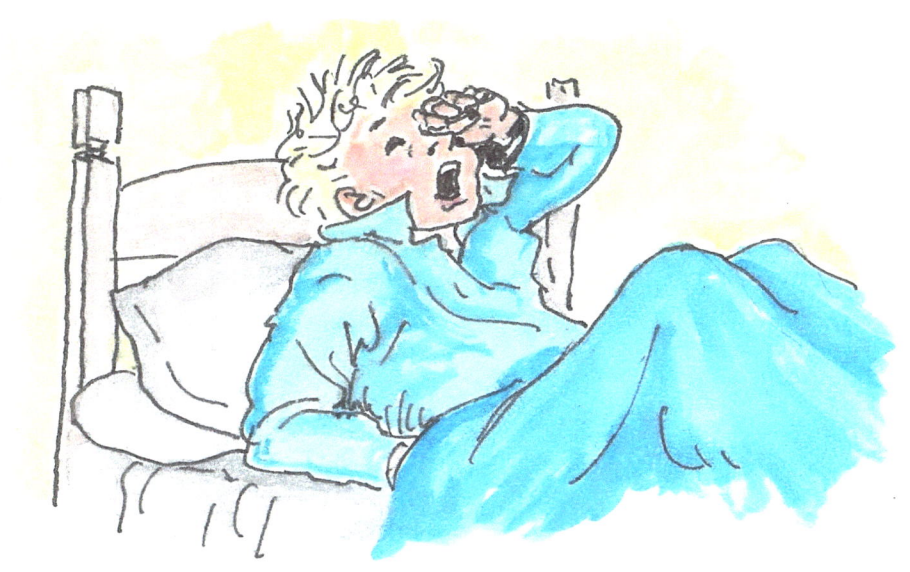

Then in the distance he heard his mom say, "TIME TO GET UP, TIME TO START YOUR DAY!"

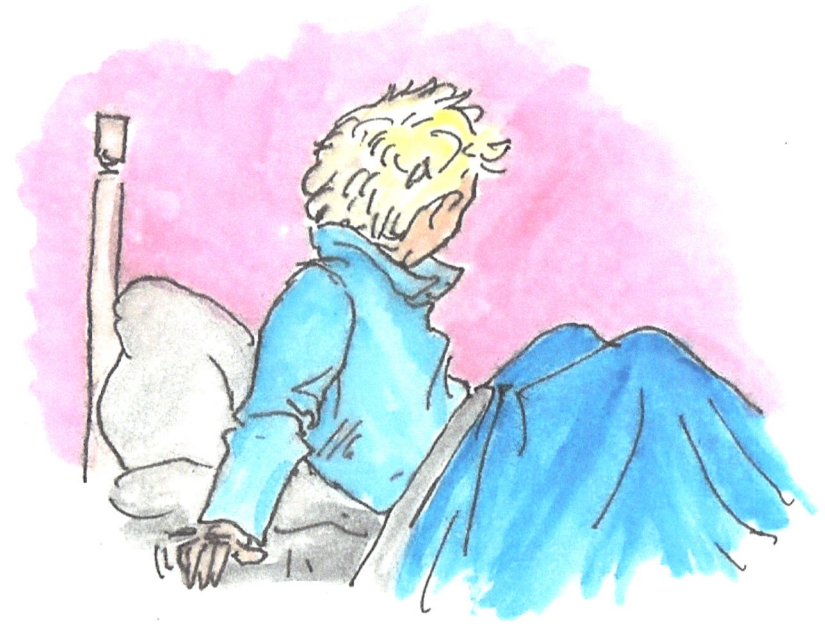

Johnny opened his eyes and then looked around, there was no monster to be seen, No FRED to be found.

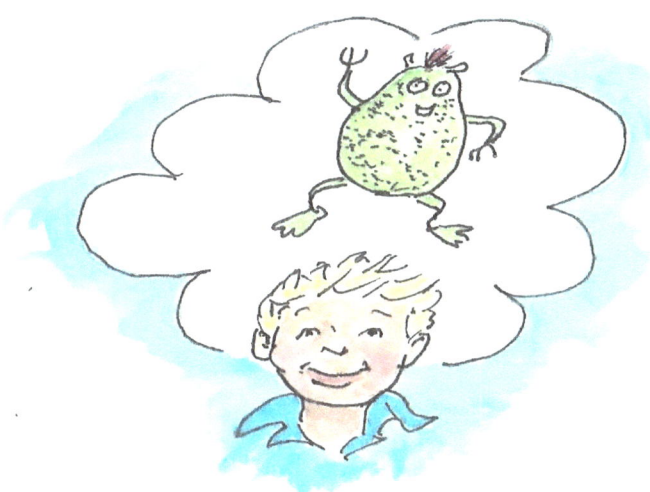

Then Johnny thought "*Where did he go, how can this be? Here was here now he's gone quick as can be.*"

Then Johnny began to laugh. "STOP PLAYING AROUND." He heard his mom scream. That's when he knew it had all been a dream.

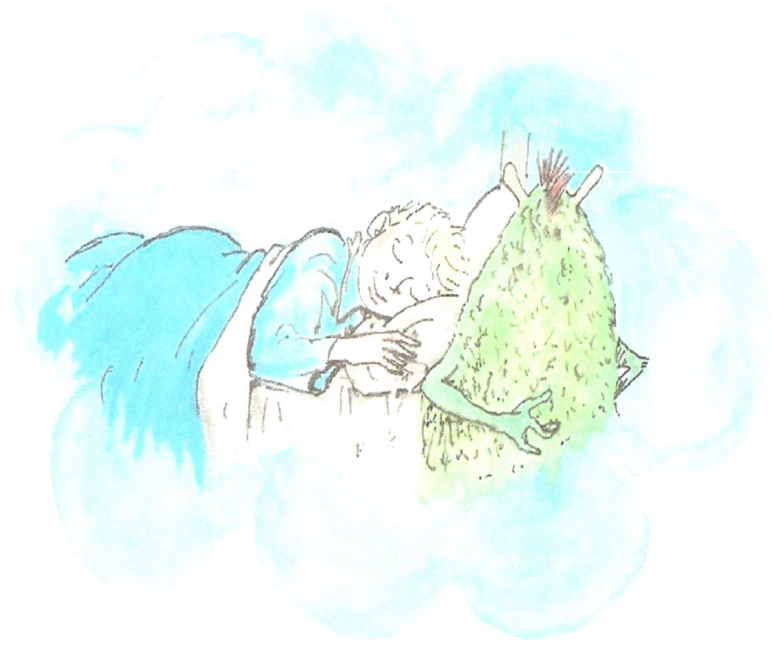

After that night Johnny always ran right up to bed. So, he could play in his dreams with his best friend FRED!

THE END

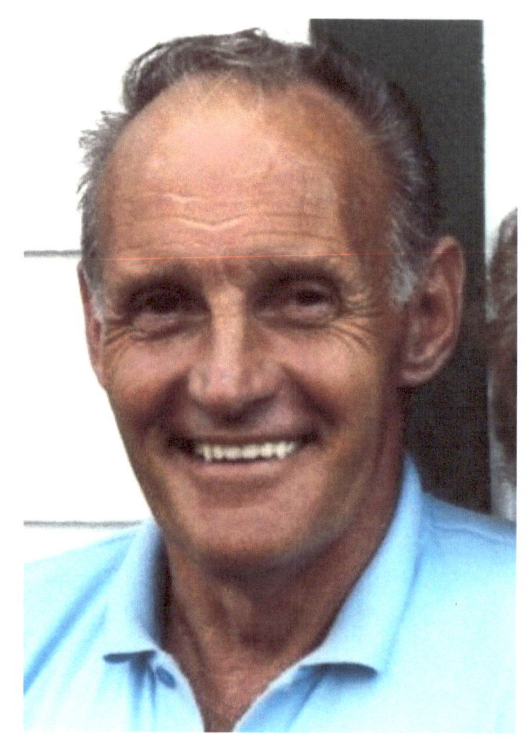

Illustrator

EARL R. FULLER

DRAW YOUR OWN IMAGINARY FRIEND

www.ingramcontent.com/pod-product-compliance
Lightning Source LLC
Chambersburg PA
CBHW050427180526
45159CB00005B/2445